SOUTH PACIFIC

Music by
Richard Rodgers

Lyrics by
Oscar Hammerstein II

Cover Photo: Mary Martin and Ezio Pinza in the original
1949 Broadway production of SOUTH PACIFIC

ISBN 978-0-88188-115-8

WILLIAMSON MUSIC®

A RODGERS AND HAMMERSTEIN COMPANY

www.williamsonmusic.com

EXCLUSIVELY DISTRIBUTED BY

HAL•LEONARD®
CORPORATION

7777 W. BLUEMOUND RD. P.O. BOX 13819 MILWAUKEE, WI 53213

Visit Hal Leonard Online at
www.halleonard.com

C O N T E N T S

Star Mary Martin with, from left to right: Co-author and director Joshua Logan; composer and co-producer Richard Rodgers; lyricist, co-author and co-producer Oscar Hammerstein II; and novelist James Michener, whose Tales of the South Pacific *provided the musical's source.*

RICHARD RODGERS & OSCAR HAMMERSTEIN II

After long and highly distinguished careers with other collaborators, Richard Rodgers (composer) and Oscar Hammerstein II (librettist/lyricist) joined forces to create the most consistently fruitful and successful partnership in the American musical theatre.

Prior to his work with Hammerstein, Richard Rodgers (1902-1979) collaborated with lyricist Lorenz Hart on a series of musical comedies that epitomized the wit and sophistication of Broadway in its heyday. Prolific on Broadway, in London and in Hollywood from the '20s into the early '40s, Rodgers & Hart wrote more than forty shows and film scores. Among their greatest were ON YOUR TOES, BABES IN ARMS, THE BOYS FROM SYRACUSE, I MARRIED AN ANGEL and PAL JOEY.

Mary Martin as Nellie Forbush in her "SeaBee" sailor outfit. Autographed to Richard Rodgers: "Dick—See! You're my honeybun today and every day— Love Mary"
Photo by Halsman

Throughout the same era Oscar Hammerstein II (1895-1960) brought new life to a moribund artform: the operetta. His collaborations with such preeminent composers as Rudolf Friml, Sigmund Romberg and Vincent Youmans resulted in such operetta classics as THE DESERT SONG, ROSE-MARIE and THE NEW MOON. With Jerome Kern he wrote SHOW BOAT, the 1927 masterpiece that changed the course of modern musical theatre. His last musical before embarking on an exclusive partnership with Richard Rodgers was CARMEN JONES, the highly-acclaimed 1943 all-black revision of Georges Bizet's tragic opera CARMEN.

OKLAHOMA!, the first Rodgers & Hammerstein musical, was also the first of a new genre, the musical play, representing a unique fusion of Rodgers' musical comedy and Hammerstein's operetta. A milestone in the development of the American musical, it also marked the beginning of the most successful partnership in Broadway musical history, and was followed by CAROUSEL, ALLEGRO, SOUTH PACIFIC, THE KING AND I, ME AND JULIET, PIPE DREAM, FLOWER DRUM SONG and THE SOUND OF MUSIC. Rodgers & Hammerstein wrote one musical specifically for the big screen, STATE FAIR, and one for television, CINDERELLA. Collectively, the Rodgers & Hammerstein musicals earned 35 Tony

United States postage stamp honoring Rodgers and Hammerstein, issued September 21, 1999.

Awards, 15 Academy Awards, two Pulitzer Prizes, two Grammy Awards and two Emmy Awards. In 1998 Rodgers & Hammerstein were cited by *Time* Magazine and CBS News as among the 20 most influential artists of the 20th century, and in 1999 they were jointly commemorated on a U.S. postage stamp.

Despite Hammerstein's death in 1960, Rodgers continued to write for the Broadway stage. His first solo entry, NO STRINGS, earned him two Tony Awards for music and lyrics, and was followed by DO I HEAR A WALTZ?, TWO BY TWO, REX and I REMEMBER MAMA. Richard Rodgers died on December 30, 1979, less than eight months after his last musical opened on Broadway. In March of 1990, Broadway's 46th Street Theatre was renamed The Richard Rodgers Theatre in his honor.

At the turn of the 21st century, the Rodgers and Hammerstein legacy continued to flourish, as marked by the enthusiasm that greeted their Centennials in 1995 and 2002.

In 1995, Hammerstein's centennial was celebrated worldwide with commemorative recordings, books, concerts and an award-winning PBS special, "Some Enchanted Evening." The ultimate tribute came the following season, when he had three musicals playing on Broadway simultaneously: SHOW BOAT (1995 Tony Award winner, Best Musical Revival); THE KING AND I (1996 Tony Award winner, Best Musical Revival); and STATE FAIR (1996 Tony Award nominee for Best Score).

SOMETHING GOOD

A Broadway Salute to Richard Rodgers on His 100th Birthday

Friday, June 28, 2002
Gershwin Theatre • New York City

In 2002, the Richard Rodgers Centennial was celebrated around the world, with tributes from Tokyo to London, from the Hollywood Bowl to the White House, featuring six new television specials, museum retrospectives, a dozen new ballets, half a dozen books, new recordings and countless concert and stage productions (including three simultaneous revivals on Broadway, matching Hammerstein's feat of six years earlier), giving testament to the enduring popularity of Richard Rodgers and the sound of his music.

Something Wonderful

A Celebration of Oscar Hammerstein II on his 100th birthday

Wednesday, July 12, 1995
Gershwin Theatre, New York

SYNOPSIS

SOUTH PACIFIC is set during World War II on a remote island in the South Pacific, where the U.S. Navy and Marines have set up a temporary base. The story begins at the home of Emile de Becque, a wealthy French planter. His two children are playing and singing outside (**"Dites-Moi"**), while inside the house, a romance is developing. Emile is having dinner with Nellie Forbush, a Navy nurse from Little Rock, Arkansas. Nellie is glad to be away from small-town life, and is making the most of her time in the South Pacific by being **"A Cockeyed Optimist."** Although they have only known each other a short while, they are already imagining privately what it would be like to be married (**"Twin Soliloquies"**). The attraction between them is very strong, and "as strange as it seems," they have fallen in love (**"Some Enchanted Evening"**). Before she leaves, Emile asks Nellie to consider the idea of marriage.

Mary Martin as Nellie Forbush, with the Nurses during "A Wonderful Guy."

Mary Martin as Nellie Forbush, washing that man right out of her hair.

Ezio Pinza as Emile de Becque, Mary Martin as Nellie Forbush.

Back at the base, the soldiers are singing about **"Bloody Mary,"** a colorful and earthy Tonkinese woman who sells items to the troops. She arouses their interest in the nearby island of Bali Ha'i, which has been declared off-limits. The local women have been evacuated there because of the war, and even though the soldiers are living on an island paradise, they all agree that **"There Is Nothin' Like a Dame."**

Lieutenant Joseph Cable is sent on a mission to gather enemy intelligence reports by infiltrating a Japanese-controlled island. But when Bloody Mary sees the handsome young officer, she plans a mission of her own—to make Cable her son-in-law. She describes **"Bali Ha'i"** to him as well, and the island's mysterious appeal piques his curiosity. But for now, his mission must take top priority. He wants to recruit the help of Emile de Becque, whose vast knowledge of the area would be a valuable asset. But first, he needs to be sure that de Becque can be trusted. Cable's superiors ask Nellie to find out everything she can about him. Nellie realizes for the first time that she really doesn't know much about Emile at all, and she begins to second-guess her feelings. Letters from home only reinforce her apprehensions about the middle-aged foreigner, and she decides that the relationship must end (**"I'm Gonna Wash That Man Right Outa My Hair"**). Her resolve is put to the test immediately when Emile suddenly appears. Remembering her duty, she steadies herself by questioning him about his past and his political beliefs. Emile convinces Nellie that her fears are unfounded, and once again she is happily in love with **"A Wonderful Guy."**

Myron McCormick as Luther Billis leads the SeaBees in "There Is Nothin' Like a Dame."

Photos from the original 1949 Broadway production

William Tabbert as Lt. Joseph Cable sings "Younger Than Springtime" to Liat (Betta St. John).

"Happy Talk": Juanita Hall as Bloody Mary, Betta St. John as Liat and William Tabbert as Lt. Joseph Cable.

"Happy Talk," he simply cannot marry Liat. Furious, Bloody Mary drags Liat away, leaving Cable bitter and heartbroken. A stage show is being presented at the base, and for the final act, Nellie dresses as a sailor and sings a boisterous showstopper (**"Honey Bun"**). As Cable reflects about his feelings for Liat, he realizes that bigotry is not something you're born with, but it is instilled in you at an early age (**"You've Got to Be Carefully Taught"**).

Emile is also brokenhearted over losing Nellie (**"This Nearly Was Mine"**). With nothing else to lose, he agrees to accompany Cable on his war mission. They reach the island successfully, and are able to provide critical information to the Allied forces, paving the way for several successful invasions. But after only a few days, Cable is killed in an attack. Nellie can only assume that Emile is also dead, and she bitterly laments the fact that she rejected him. Overcoming her prejudices, she goes to his house to comfort his children. Emile returns safely. The past forgotten, they can now begin their life together.

Based on Nellie's information, Emile is asked to accompany Cable on his mission to establish a spy post on the island of Marie-Louise. But Emile is not willing to risk his life to help the Americans; his future with Nellie is more important to him than anything else. The operation is too dangerous without Emile's expertise, so it has to be put on hold. While Cable waits for his next orders, he takes the opportunity to visit Bali Ha'i. Bloody Mary arranges for him to meet her seventeen-year-old daughter, Liat. It is love at first sight, and Cable finds it difficult to return to the base (**"Younger Than Springtime"**). Meanwhile, Emile finally works up the courage to share with Nellie part of his past he has not yet revealed: his late Polynesian wife and their two Eurasian children. Nellie is unable to overcome the prejudices from her conservative southern upbringing, and decides that she must never see Emile again.

As Act II begins, Bloody Mary gives Cable an ultimatum to marry Liat. Like Nellie, he too was raised with racial prejudice, and despite Bloody Mary's

The final scene: Emile de Becque (Ezio Pinza) and Nellie Forbush (Mary Martin) are reunited, as the children (BarBara Luna as Ngana, and Michael DeLeon as Jerome) look on.

*Note: **"My Girl Back Home"** was cut from the original score, but was used in the 1958 film version.*

THE TALE OF
SOUTH PACIFIC

The tale of SOUTH PACIFIC is as fascinating as the "tales" that inspired it.

When director Joshua Logan suggested the idea of doing a musical based on James Michener's collection of short stories, *Tales of the South Pacific*, to producer Leland Hayward, Hayward immediately saw its possibilities. Logan, who had already achieved great success in the post-World War II theatre with his production of MISTER ROBERTS, saw great dramatic potential in focusing on one corner of the vast world war that had just been fought. He conveyed his vision to longtime friend and collaborator, composer Richard Rodgers.

Rodgers thought that several of the stories had strong dramatic potential, and his opinion was confirmed by his partner, librettist/lyricist Oscar Hammerstein II. (Hammerstein also consulted with his son, William Hammerstein, who had not only been the stage manager for Logan's war-time drama MISTER ROBERTS, but had himself served with the U.S. Navy in the South Pacific.) While Logan had originally intended to musicalize only one of the stories in Michener's collection, "Fo' Dolla," it was Rodgers' idea that they secure rights to the entire book to draw different characters and plot strands for their musical. This turned out to be a wise move because, upon closer investigation, the romance at the heart of "Fo' Dolla"— about a handsome American Marine officer and the local island girl whose heart he breaks—was too close to Puccini's MADAME BUTTERFLY to build an entire musical around (at least, such was the thinking in the days before MISS SAIGON). So, while it was decided to make this the tragic subplot of the musical, another romance was needed to give SOUTH PACIFIC its dramatic structure. A story called "Our Heroine" seemed a better choice for a main plot, and its unusual May-December romance was perfectly suited to Rodgers and Hammerstein's penchant for writing to challenging situations. This story dealt with a romance between a middle-aged French planter, Emile de Becque, and Nellie Forbush, a young American nurse from Little Rock, Arkansas. It also delved into the disturbing issue of racial intolerance and bigotry.

Director and co-author Joshua Logan, with co-producers Richard Rodgers (composer) and Oscar Hammerstein II (co-author, lyricist)

Casting the starring roles was comparatively easy. Ezio Pinza, the famed Metropolitan Opera basso, was anxious to appear in a Broadway musical and the part of Emile was perfectly suited for him. Mary Martin— who had impressed Rodgers and Hammerstein the year before with her fresh, down-home country appeal in the title role for their national tour of Irving Berlin's ANNIE GET YOUR GUN—was their first and only choice for Nellie. Martin, however, needed some coaxing; she was dying to appear in the musical, but nervous about co-starring with a vocal talent as large as Ezio Pinza's. "What do you want," she reportedly quipped. "Two basses?" But one hearing of the score convinced her. Knowing who they wanted for their leads, Rodgers and Hammerstein wrote the score for them. Thus, the two stars are never in musical competition with each other; in fact, rarely do they

Mary Martin as Nellie Forbush,
Ezio Pinza as Emile de Becque

sing a duet with one another (a reprise of "A Cock-Eyed Optimist" is the only exception, while their "Twin Soliloquies" are more complementary than competing). Emile, the romantic European, is given such luxuriant, roiling numbers as "Some Enchanted Evening" and "This Nearly Was Mine," while Nellie from Little Rock gets the infectious Broadway sounds of "A Wonderful Guy," "I'm Gonna Wash That Man Right Outa My Hair" and "Honey Bun."

SOUTH PACIFIC enjoyed a comparatively smooth sail to Broadway via out-of-town tryouts in New Haven and Boston. Expectations were running high: the director and the authors were at the pinnacles of their careers; the two stars each had fans in their own arenas and together promised to create a whole new following; and the subject matter hit home to an America still reeling from the excitement and relief at having survived a second world war in less than half a century.

By the time it opened in New York on April 7, 1949, SOUTH PACIFIC was already legendary—the major theatrical event of Broadway in its golden era. Astonishingly, this was one musical that managed not only to meet its hype, but to top it. "Magnificent!" cheered Brooks Atkinson in the *New York Times*. "SOUTH PACIFIC is as lively, warm, fresh and beautiful as we had all hoped it would be!"

SOUTH PACIFIC received the 1950 Pulitzer Prize for Drama, and for the first time the committee included a composer (Richard Rodgers) in that citation. It received nine Tony Awards (including Best Musical), the New York Drama Critics Circle Award, a Grammy Award, a Gold Record, and countless other accolades. Simultaneous with its Broadway run of 1949–54, a U.S. National Tour took SOUTH PACIFIC to 118 cities over five years. The first London production, at the venerable Theatre Royal, Drury Lane, featured Mary Martin in her Tony-winning Broadway performance. (Her son, Larry Hagman, appeared in the ensemble and was joined, later in the run, by a young Scottish actor named Sean Connery.) The 1958 motion picture version, filmed on the Hawaiian island of Kauai, starred Mitzi Gaynor and Rossano Brazzi (with the singing voice of Giorgio Tozzi.)

Over 25,000 productions of SOUTH PACIFIC have been seen worldwide since 1949, from New York City Opera revivals to countless high school and summer stock productions. Popular in the U.S., Canada, Britain, Australia and South Africa, it has also been translated for local-language versions in Sweden, Spain, Turkey, Denmark, Germany and Austria. Other noteworthy productions in recent years include Gemma Craven and Emile Belcourt in a 1988 London revival that also toured Japan; Robert Goulet in a two-year U.S. record-breaking national tour; Kiri Te Kanawa and Jose Carreras heading an all-star CBS Masterworks studio recording (also featuring Mandy Patinkin and Sarah Vaughan, conducted by Jonathan Tunick); a 1993 Australian national tour, starring Paige O'Hara, Andre Jobin and Roz Ryan; a 1997 studio cast album starring Justino Diaz and Paige O'Hara. A television movie remake for ABC-TV, starring Glenn Close as Nellie Forbush, Rade Sherbedgia as Emile and Harry Connick Jr. as Lt. Cable, was filmed on location in the South Pacific and premiered in March of 2001. In December of that year, the Royal National Theatre of Great Britain staged SOUTH PACIFIC, directed by Trevor Nunn and choreographed by Matthew Bourne. At this writing, an all-star concert version of the musical is scheduled for Carnegie Hall, New York City, in June, 2005.

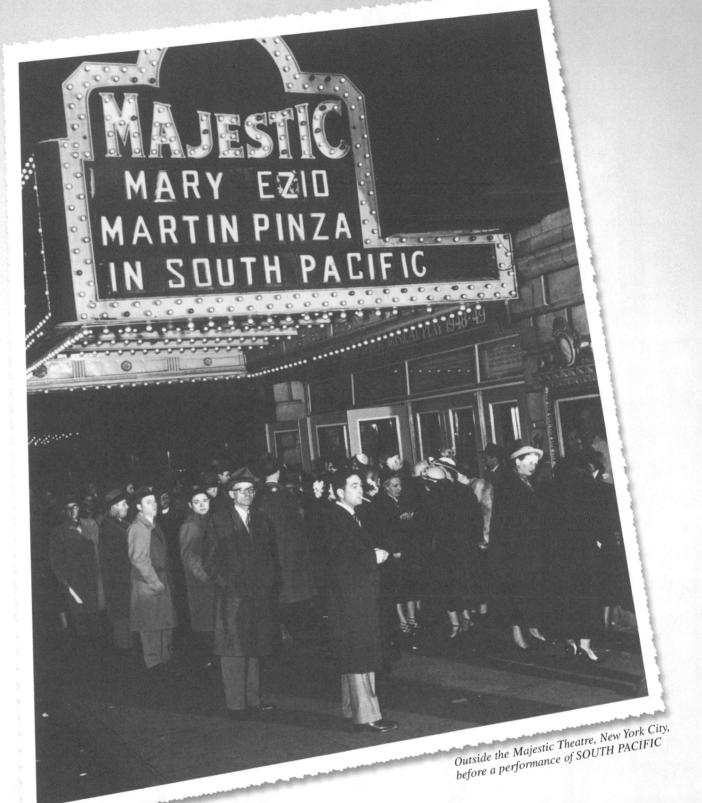

Outside the Majestic Theatre, New York City, before a performance of SOUTH PACIFIC

...And there's yet one more tale in this SOUTH PACIFIC:

On April 7, 1999, over 30 members of the original Broadway company of SOUTH PACIFIC gathered in New York City for a 50th Anniversary reunion, where they dedicated a year-long exhibit on the musical at the Museum of the City of New York; took a historic curtain call at the Majestic Theatre exactly 50 years to the day of the musical's premiere at that theatre, as the audience of the current reigning hit, *The Phantom of the Opera*, greeted them with a standing ovation; held a reunion supper at Sardi's; and attended a sold-out retrospective, *Some Enchanted Evening*, at New York's Symphony Space. It was "SOUTH PACIFIC Day" in New York City, by Mayoral decree—and it was "SOUTH PACIFIC Day" in Little Rock, Arkansas, too.

A few weeks later, still reliving that momentous 50th anniversary curtain call, one original cast member said, "As I stood on the stage of the Majestic Theatre I felt 50 years fade away...We were all young again, and involved in the musical of the century."

BALI HA'I

Lyrics by OSCAR HAMMERSTEIN II
Music by RICHARD RODGERS

Most peo-ple live on a lone-ly is - land _____

Lost in the mid-dle of a fog-gy sea. _____

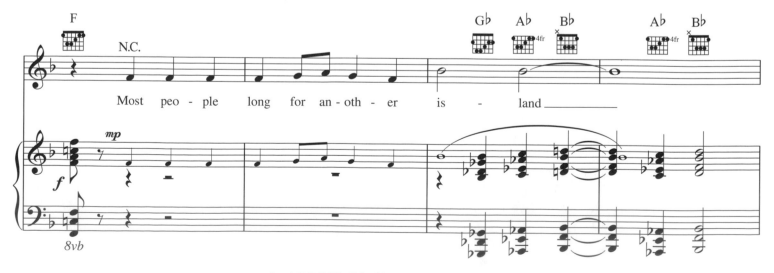

Most peo-ple long for an-oth-er is - land _____

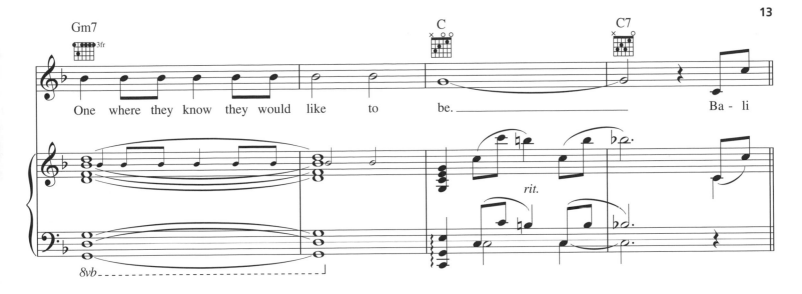

One where they know they would like to be. _____ Ba - li

Refrain *(slowly)*

Ha'i may call you an - y night, An - y day. In your

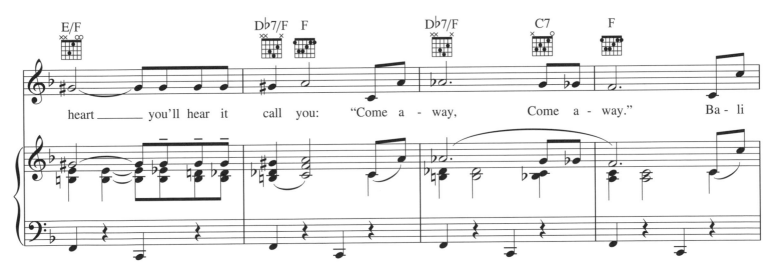

heart _____ you'll hear it call you: "Come a - way, Come a - way." Ba - li

Ha'i will whis - per On the wind of the sea: "Here am

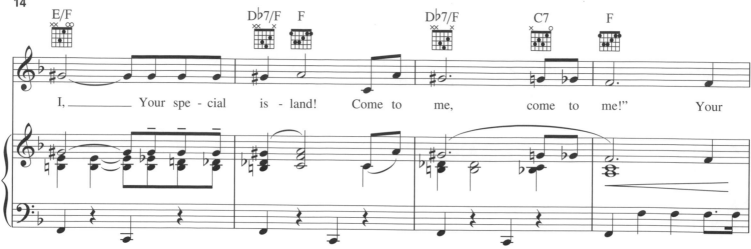

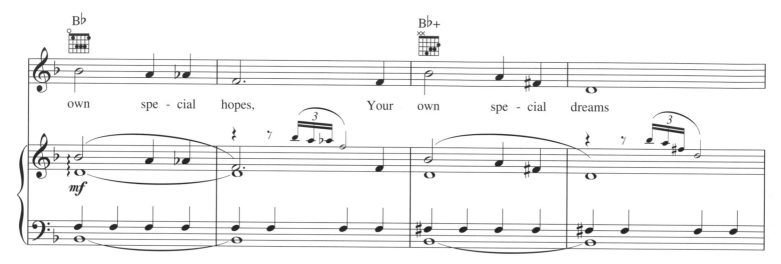

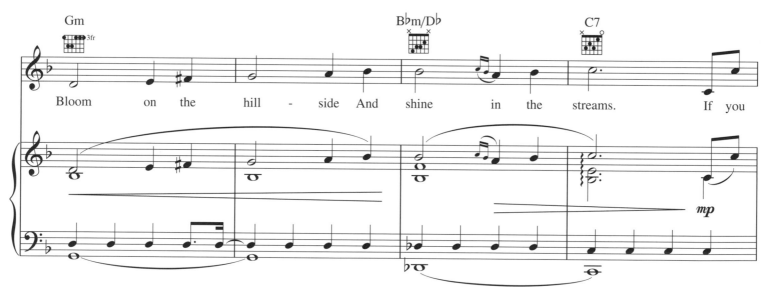

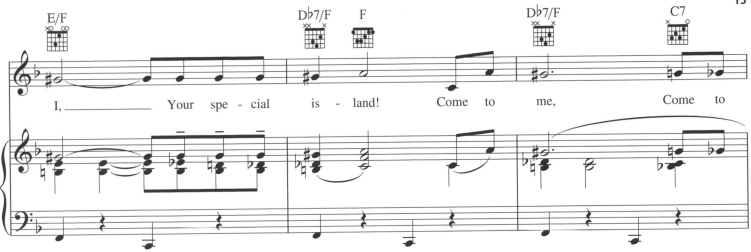

I, _____ Your spe - cial is - land! Come to me, Come to

me!" Ba - li Ha'i, Ba - li Ha'i, Ba - li

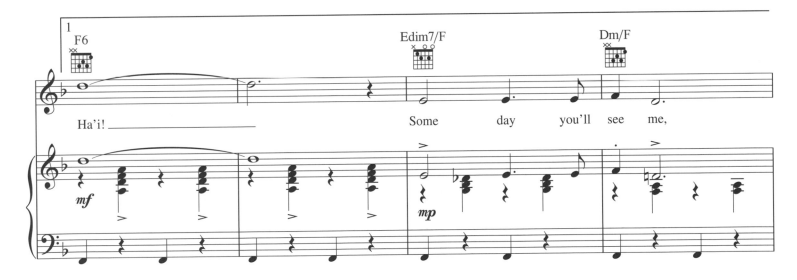

Ha'i! _____ Some day you'll see me,

Float - ing in the sun - shine, My head stick - ing out From a low - fly - ing

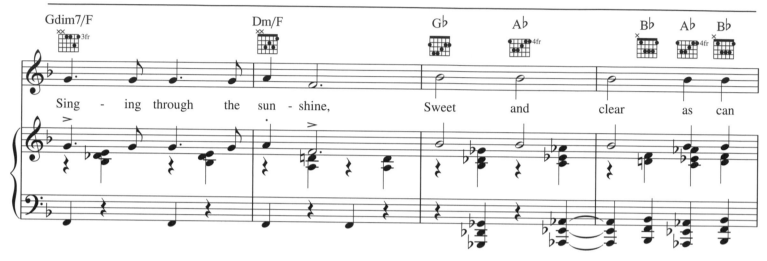

A COCKEYED OPTIMIST

Lyrics by OSCAR HAMMERSTEIN II
Music by RICHARD RODGERS

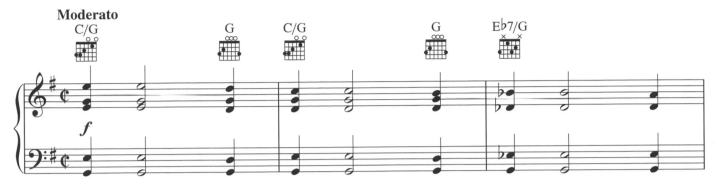

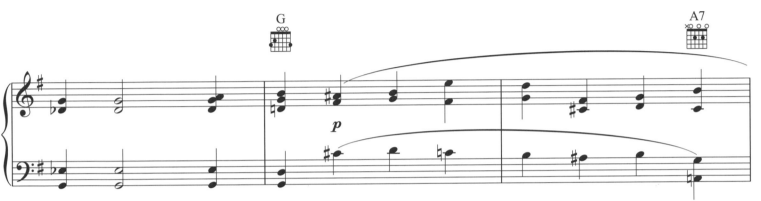

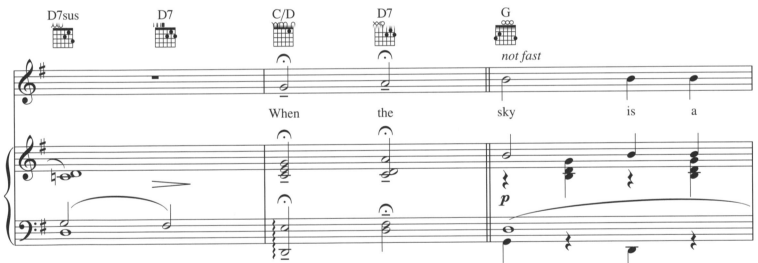

When the sky is a

bright ca-nar-y yel - low _____ I for -

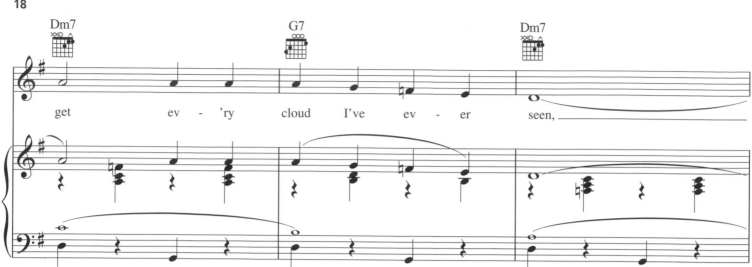

get ev - 'ry cloud I've ev - er seen,

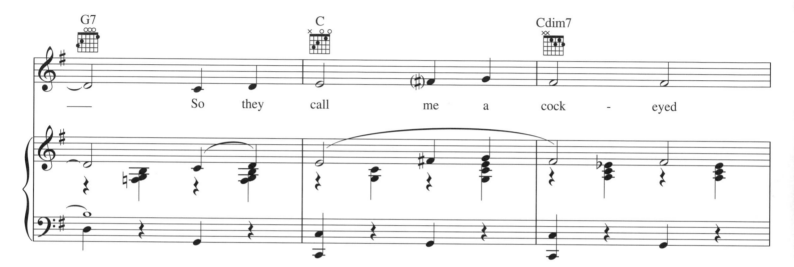

So they call me a cock - eyed

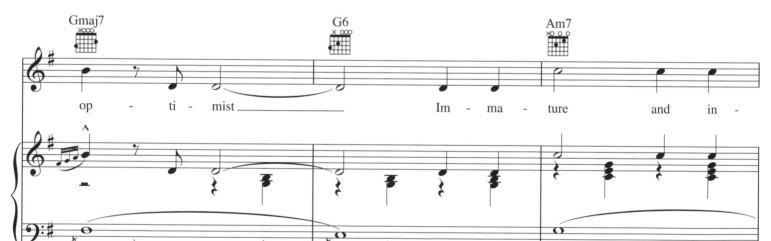

op - ti - mist Im - ma - ture and in -

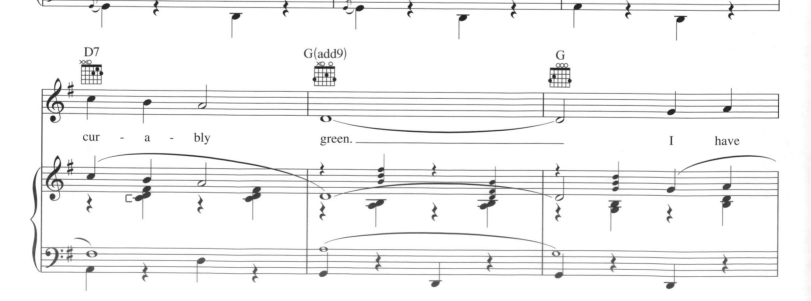

cur - a - bly green. I have

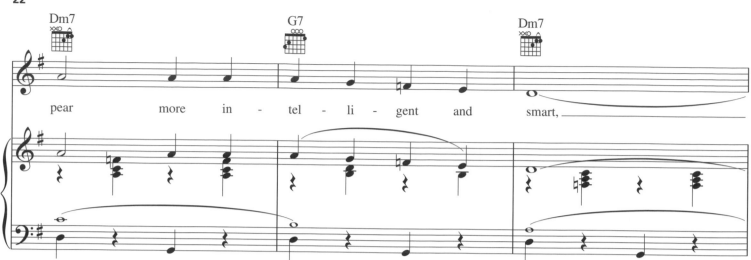

pear   more   in - tel - li - gent   and   smart, _____

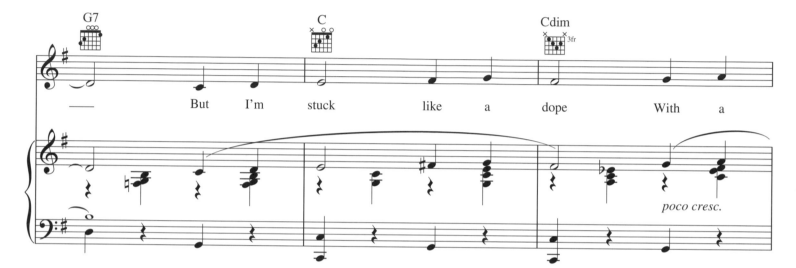

_____   But   I'm   stuck   like   a   dope   With   a

poco cresc.

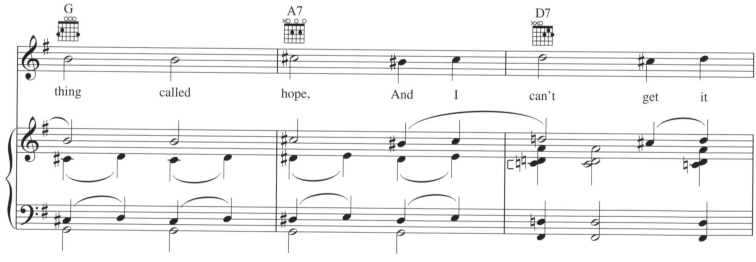

thing   called   hope,   And   I   can't   get   it

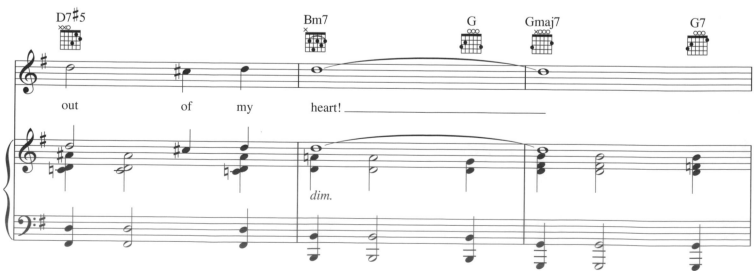

out   of   my   heart! _____

dim.

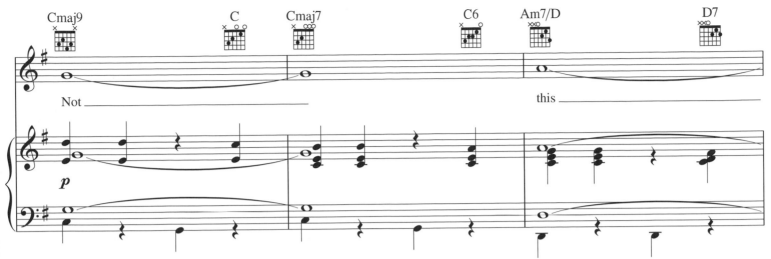

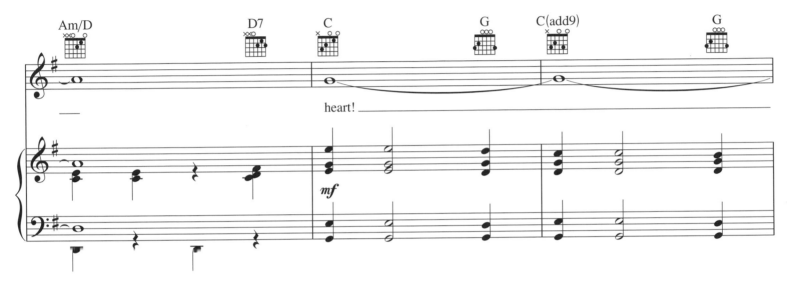

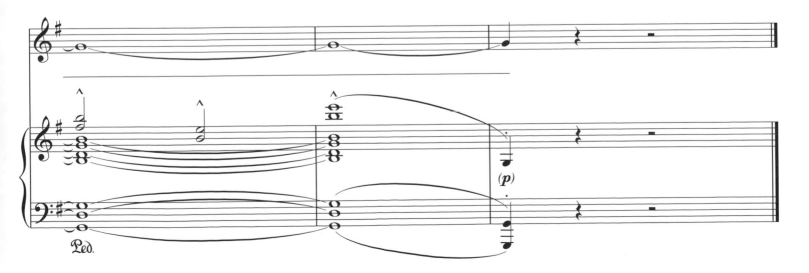

BLOODY MARY

Lyrics by OSCAR HAMMERSTEIN II
Music by RICHARD RODGERS

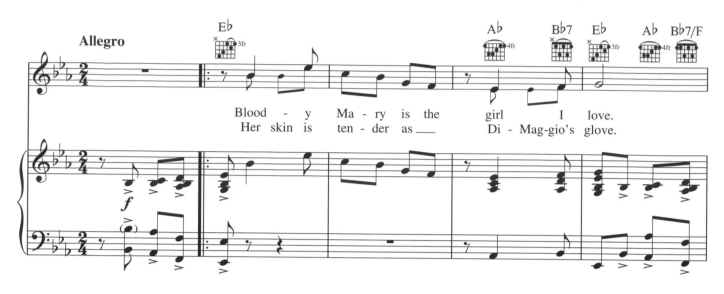

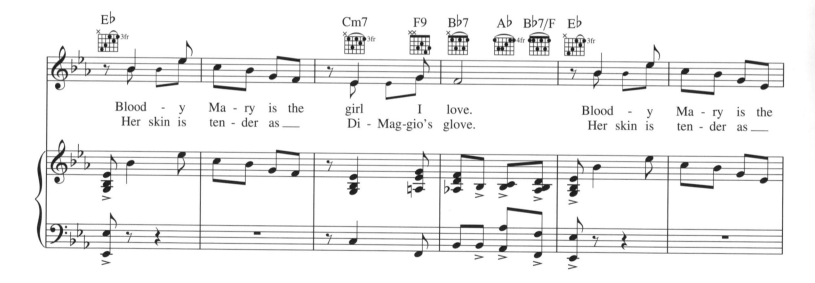

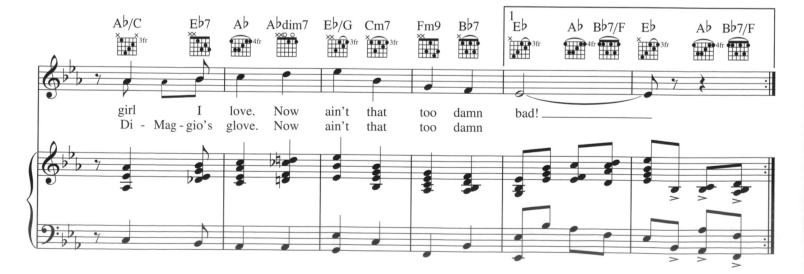

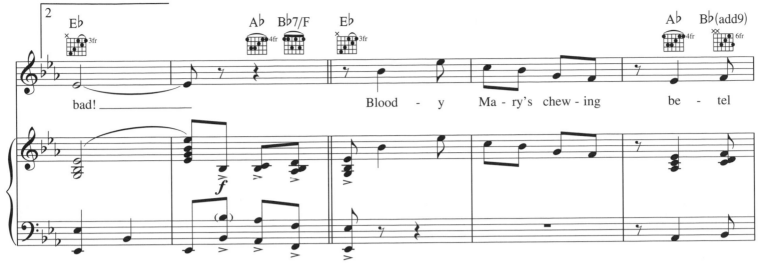

bad! _____ Blood - y Ma - ry's chew-ing be - tel

nuts, She is al - ways chew - ing be - tel nuts,

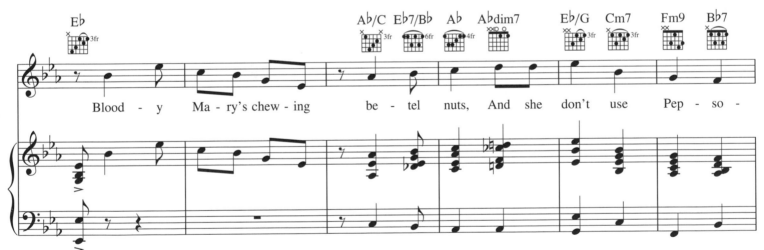

Blood - y Ma - ry's chew - ing be - tel nuts, And she don't use Pep - so -

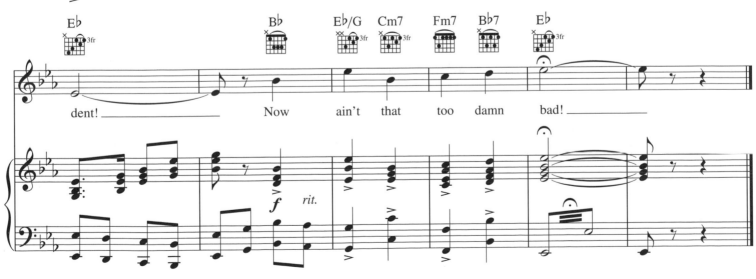

dent! _____ Now ain't that too damn bad! _____

DITES-MOI
(Tell Me Why)

Lyrics by OSCAR HAMMERSTEIN II
Music by RICHARD RODGERS

Moderato e semplice

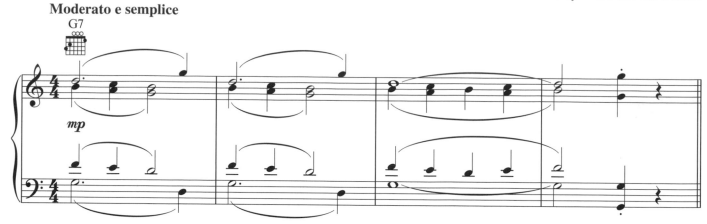

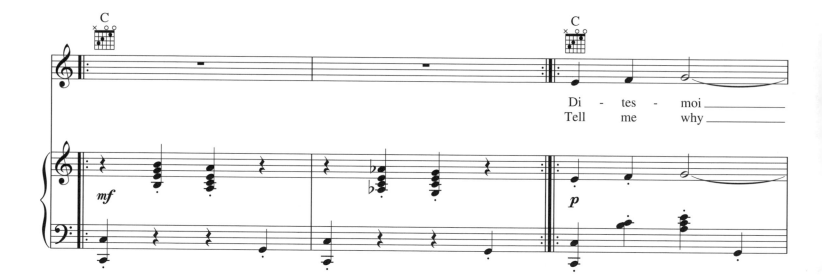

Di - tes - moi _____
Tell me why _____

_____ Pour - quoi _____ La vie est bel - le,
_____ The sky _____ is filled with mu - sic,

Di - tes - moi _____ Pour - quoi _____ La vie est
Tell me why _____ We fly _____ on clouds a -

C

gai? Di - tes - moi _____ Pour - quoi, _____
bove Can it be _____ that we _____

C7　　　　　　　　　　F　　　　　　Cdim

_____ Chère ma - d'moi - sel - le, Est - ce - que
_____ can fly to mu - sic Just be - cause,

poco rit.　　　　　　　　　　　　　　　delicat
　　　　　　　　　　　　　　　　　　　　mp

C　　　　　　F6　　G7　　1 C　　G7　　2 C

Par - ce - que vous m'ai - mez? mez?
Just be - cause we're in love? love?

p

HAPPY TALK

Lyrics by OSCAR HAMMERSTEIN II
Music by RICHARD RODGERS

Allegretto grazioso

Refrain

1. & 2. Refrain Hap - py talk, keep talk - in'

hap - py talk,_____ Talk a - bout things you'd

like to do. _____ You

got-ta have a dream, ___ If you don't have a dream ___

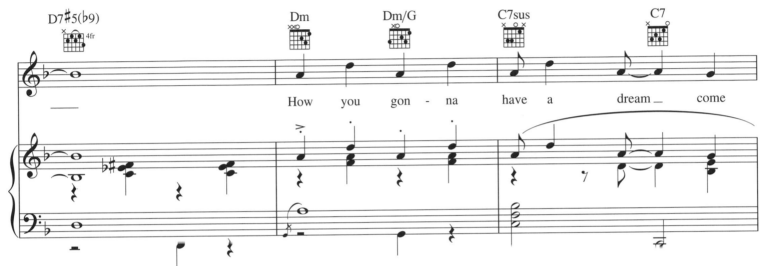

How you gon-na have a dream ___ come

true? _____

Verse

Talk a - bout a moon
Talk a - bout a star

Float - in' in de sky, Look - in' like a
Look - in' like a toy, Peek - in' through de

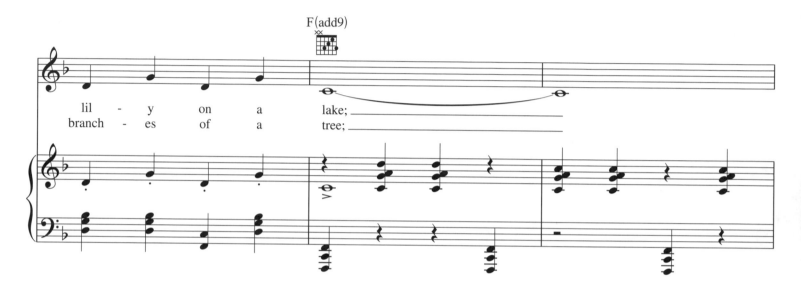

lil - y on a lake;
branch - es of a tree;

Talk a - bout a bird Learn - in' how to
Talk a - bout a girl Talk a - bout a

fly Mak - in' all de mu - sic he can
boy Count - in' all de rip - ples on de

hap - py talk, _____ Talk a - bout things you'd

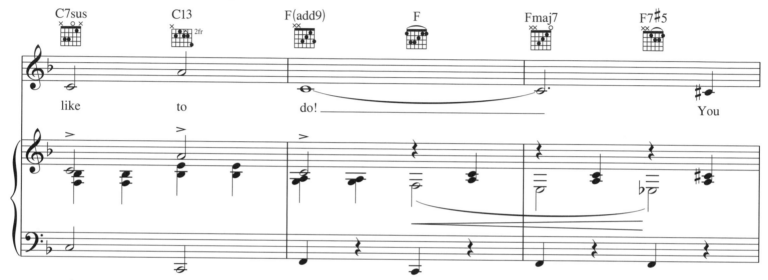

like to do! _____ You

got - ta have a dream, ___ If you don't have a dream _

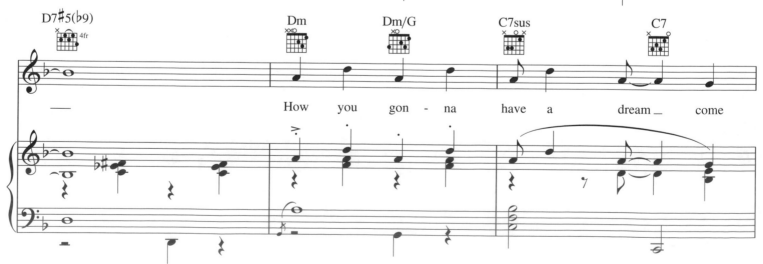

___ How you gon - na have a dream _ come

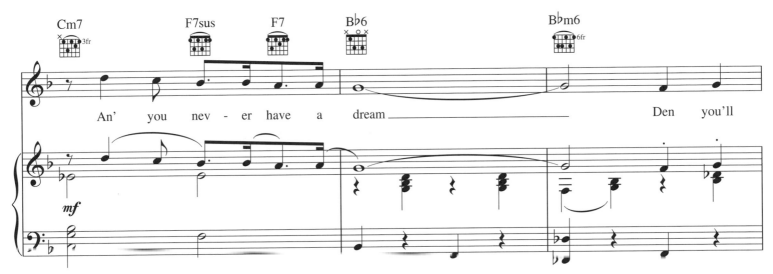

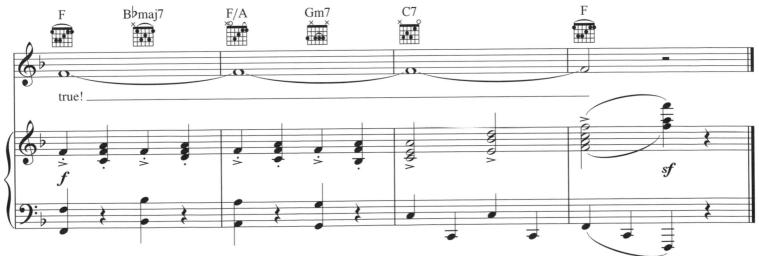

HONEY BUN

Lyrics by OSCAR HAMMERSTEIN II
Music by RICHARD RODGERS

Refrain *(lively)*

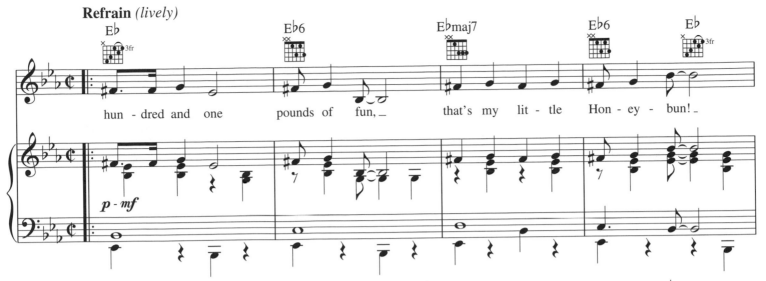

hun - dred and one pounds of fun, _ that's my lit - tle Hon - ey - bun! _

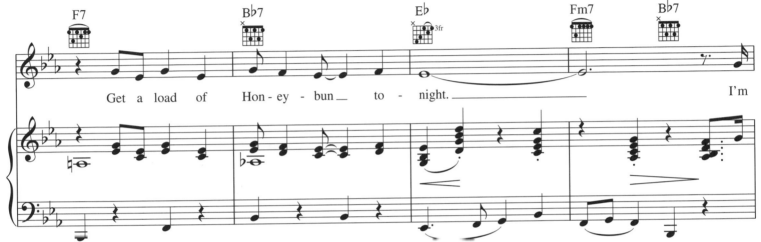

Get a load of Hon - ey - bun _ to - night. _____ I'm

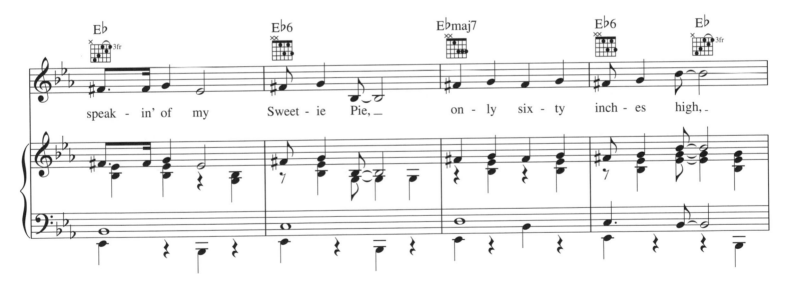

speak - in' of my Sweet - ie Pie, _ on - ly six - ty inch - es high, _

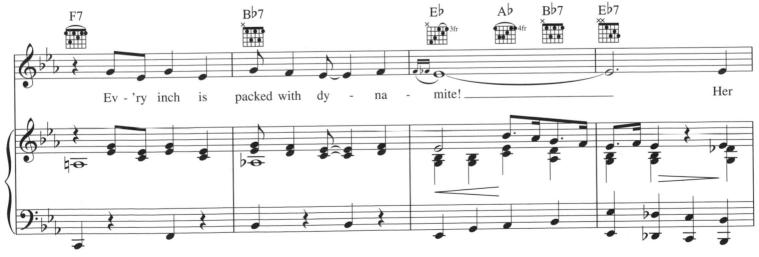

Ev - 'ry inch is packed with dy - na - mite! _____ Her

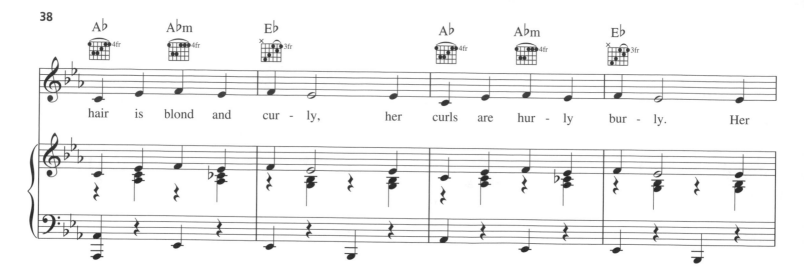

hair is blond and cur - ly, her curls are hur - ly bur - ly. Her

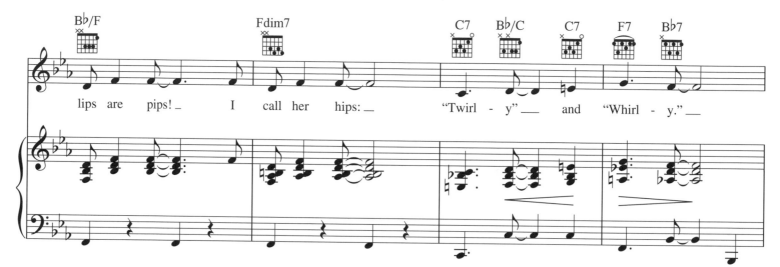

lips are pips! __ I call her hips: __ "Twirl - y" __ and "Whirl - y." __

She's my ba - by, I'm her pap! __ I'm her boob - y, she's my trap! __

I am caught and I don't want - a run __ 'cause I'm hav - in' so much fun with Hon - ey -

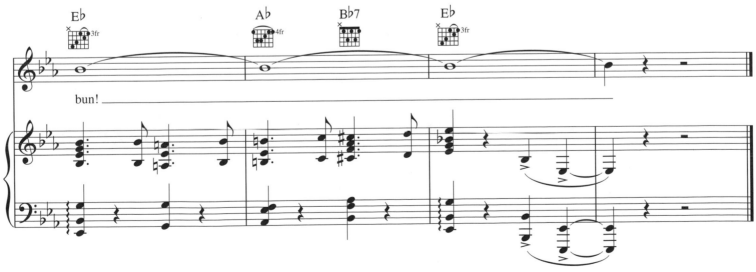

I'M GONNA WASH THAT MAN RIGHT OUTA MY HAIR

Lyrics by OSCAR HAMMERSTEIN II
Music by RICHARD RODGERS

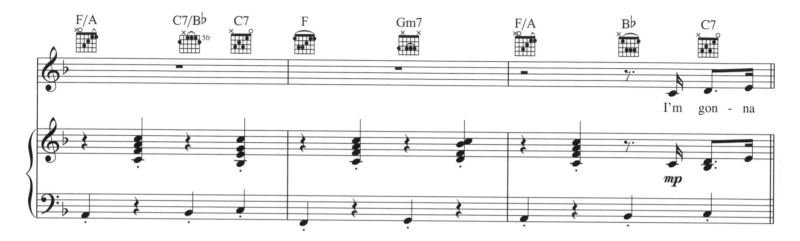

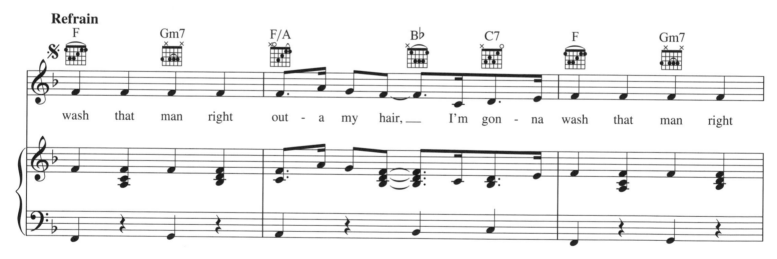

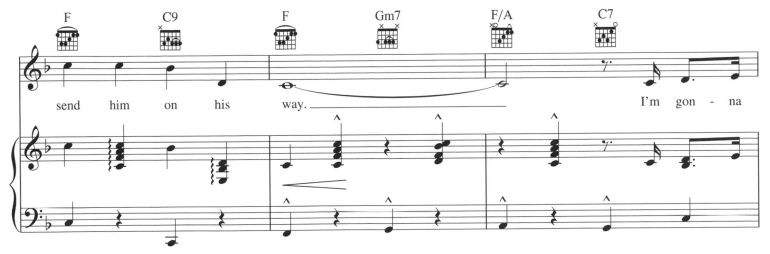

send him on his way. _____ I'm gon - na

wave that man right out - a my arms, _ I'm gon - na wave that man right

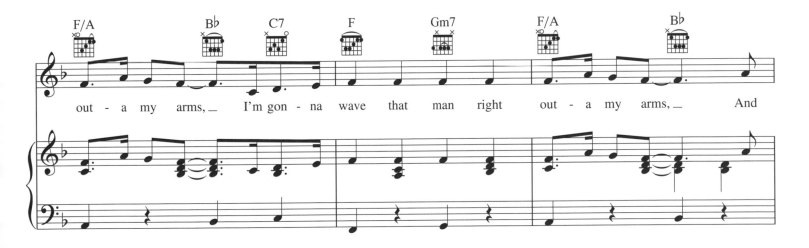

out - a my arms, _ I'm gon-na wave that man right out - a my arms, _ And

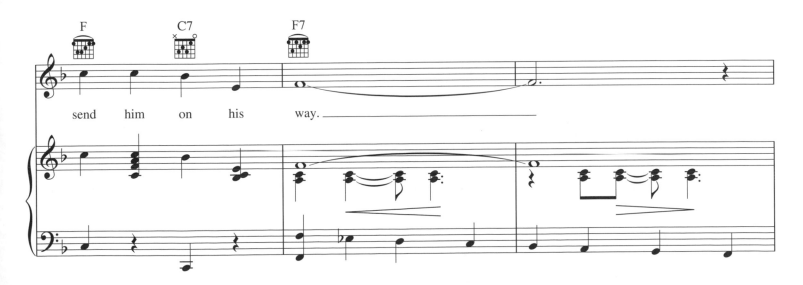

send him on his way. _____

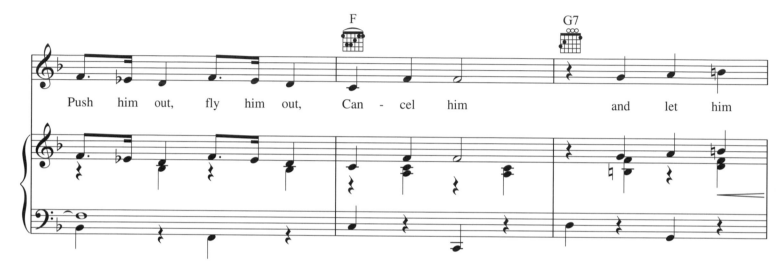

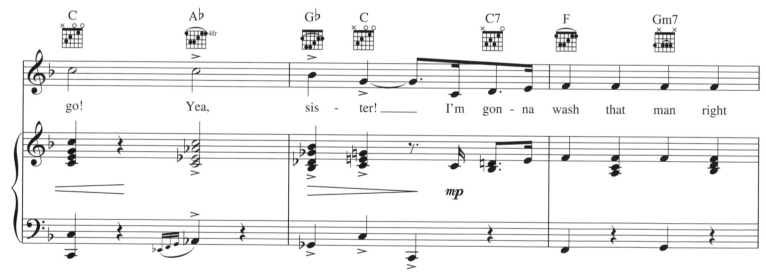

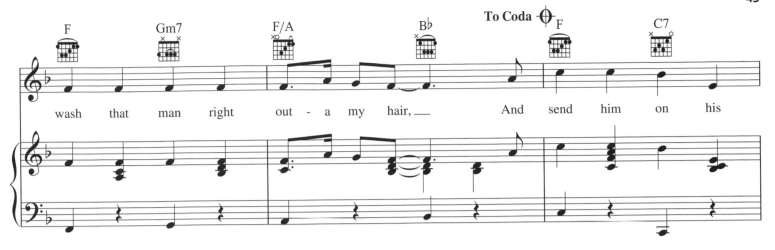

wash that man right out - a my hair, ___ And send him on his

Interlude

way. If the man don't un - der - stand you ___ If you

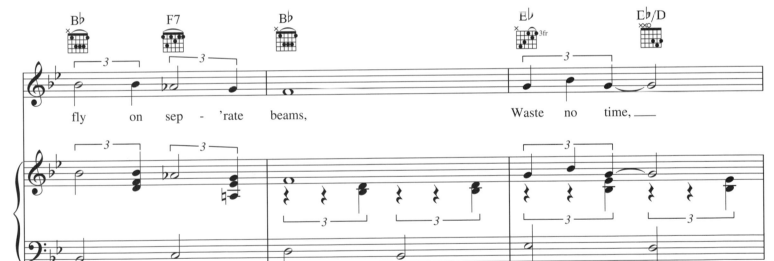

fly on sep - 'rate beams, Waste no time, ___

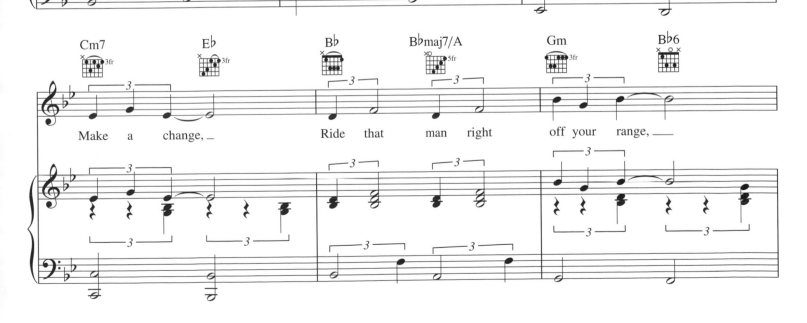

Make a change, ___ Ride that man right off your range, ___

Rub him out - a the roll - call _____ And drum him out - a your dreams. If you laugh at dif - f'rent com - ics _____ If you root for dif - f'rent teams, Waste no time, ___

Weep no more, ___ Show him what the door is for! ___

MY GIRL BACK HOME

Lyrics by OSCAR HAMMERSTEIN II
Music by RICHARD RODGERS

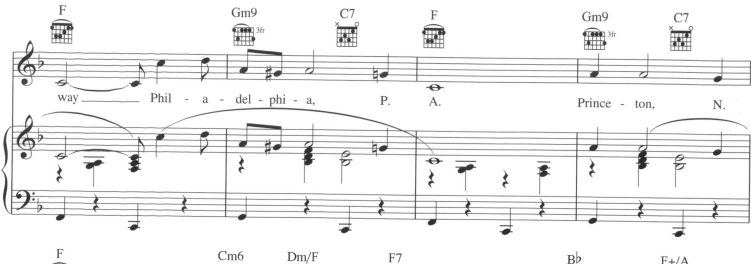

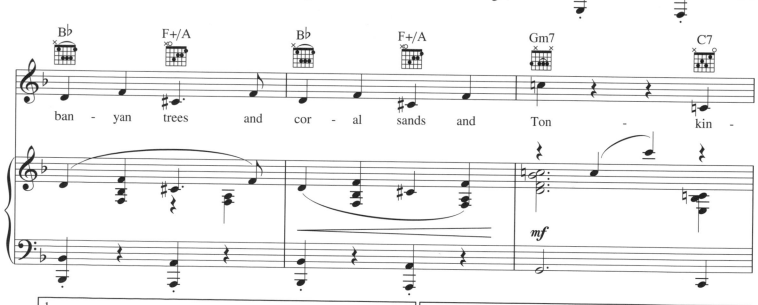

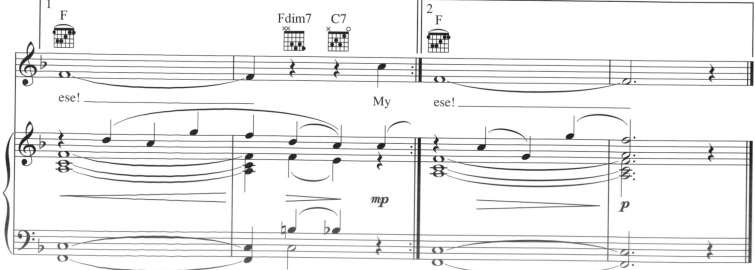

SOME ENCHANTED EVENING

Lyrics by OSCAR HAMMERSTEIN II
Music by RICHARD RODGERS

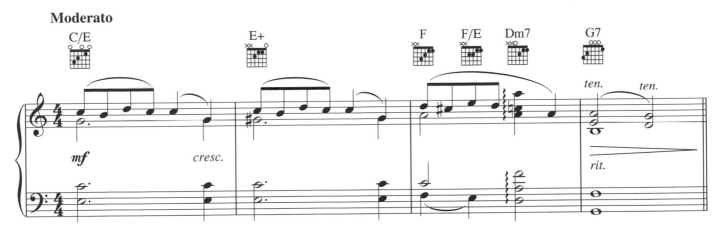

Some en-chant-ed eve-ning ___ You may see a stran-ger,___

You may see a stran-ger ___ A-cross a

side ____ And make her your own, ____ Or all through your

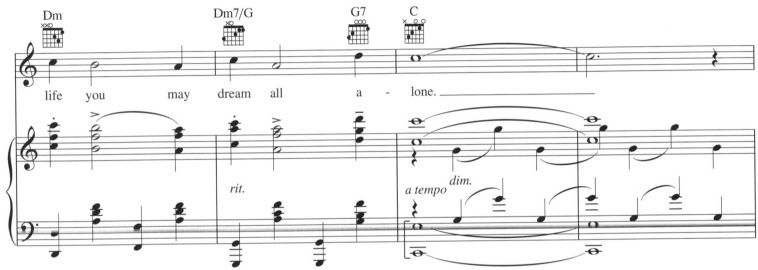

life you may dream all a - lone. ____

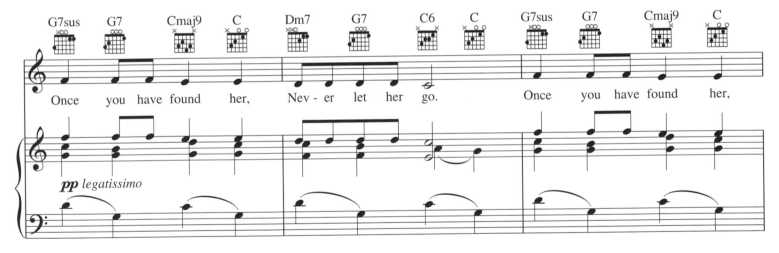

Once you have found her, Nev - er let her go. Once you have found her,

Nev - er let her go! ____

THERE IS NOTHIN' LIKE A DAME

Lyrics by OSCAR HAMMERSTEIN II
Music by RICHARD RODGERS

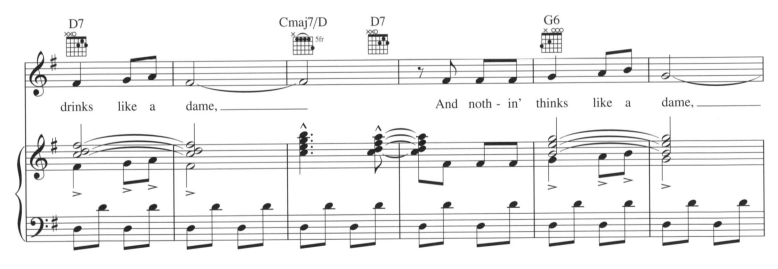

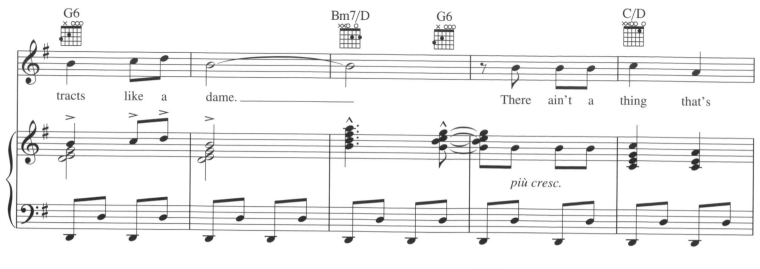

tracts like a dame. _____ There ain't a thing that's

wrong with an - y man here That can't be cured by

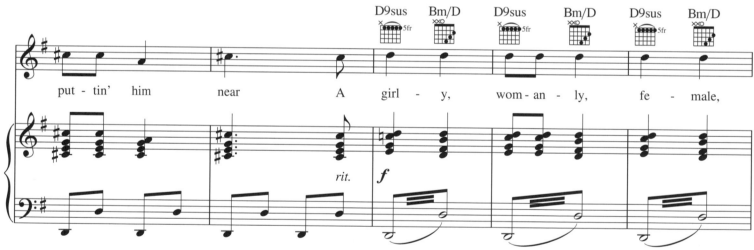

put - tin' him near A girl - y, wom - an - ly, fe - male,

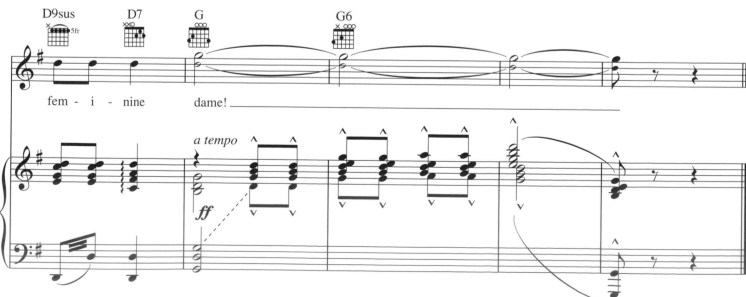

fem - i - nine dame! _____

TWIN SOLILOQUIES
(This Is How It Feels)

Lyrics by OSCAR HAMMERSTEIN II
Music by RICHARD RODGERS

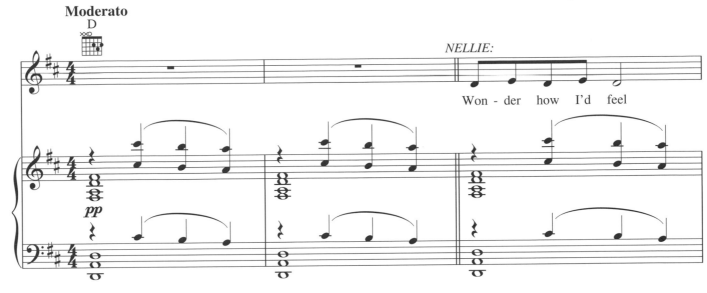

NELLIE:
Won - der how I'd feel

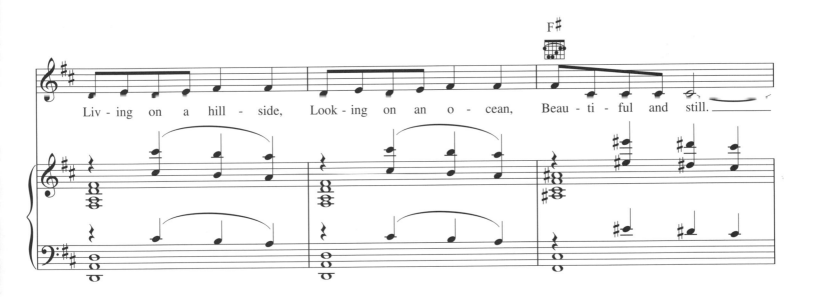

Liv - ing on a hill - side, Look - ing on an o - cean, Beau - ti - ful and still.

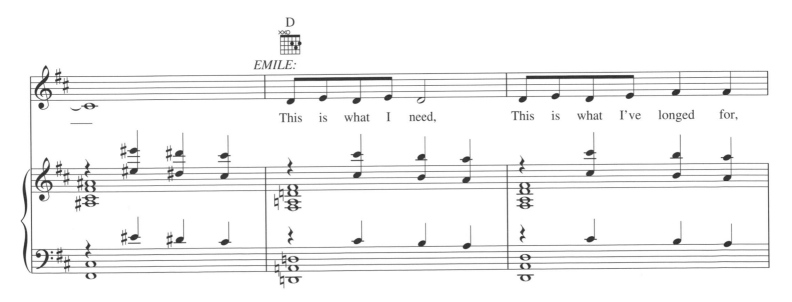

EMILE:
This is what I need, This is what I've longed for,

Some - one young and smil - ing Climb - ing up my hill! _____

NELLIE:

We are not a - like. Prob - a - bly I'd bore him. He's a cul - tured French - man,

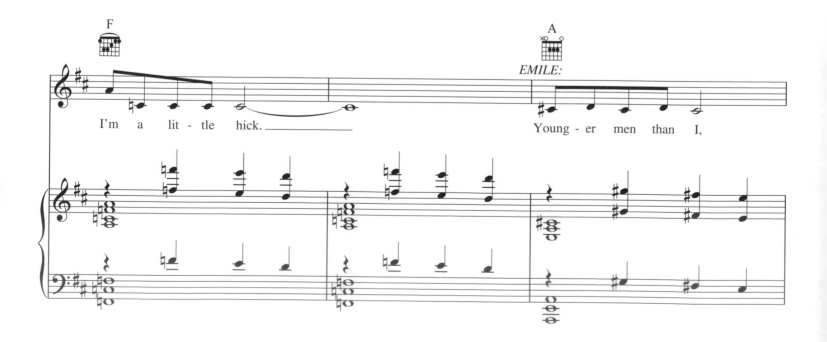

I'm a lit - tle hick. _____

EMILE:

Young - er men than I,

Of - fi - cers and doc - tors, Prob - a - bly pur - sue her, she could have her pick. ____

Allegro

NELLIE:

Won - der why I feel Jit - ter - y and

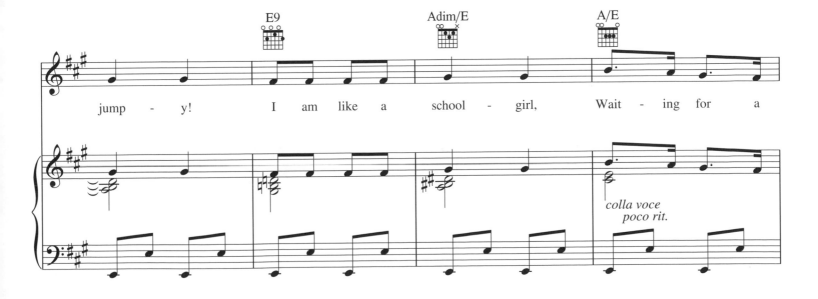

jump - y! I am like a school - girl, Wait - ing for a

colla voce
poco rit.

EMILE:

dance. Can I ask her now? I am like a school - boy!

What will be her an - swer? Do I have a

Optional Ending

chance? _____

poco a poco cresc.

F/G

F#m6

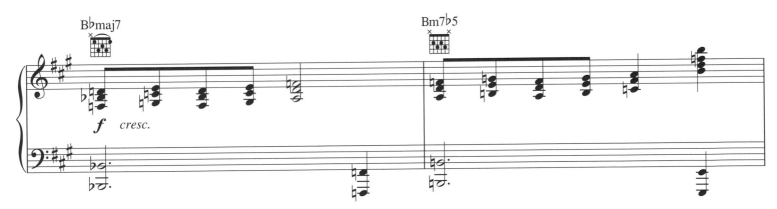

Bbmaj7   Bm7b5

f cresc.

A

ff

THIS NEARLY WAS MINE

Lyrics by OSCAR HAMMERSTEIN II
Music by RICHARD RODGERS

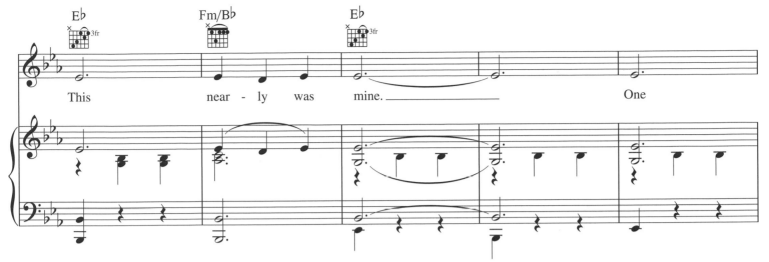

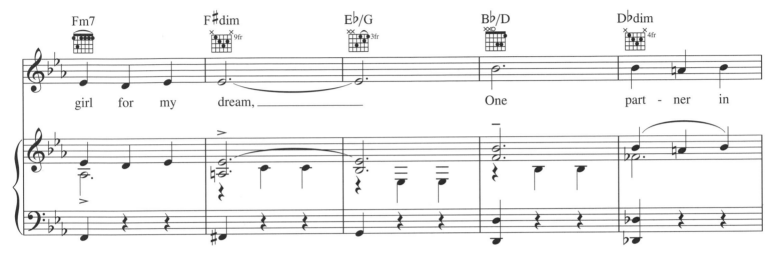

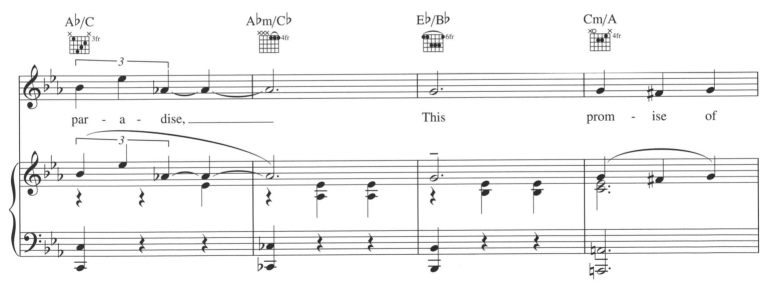

mine. _____ Close to my heart she came _____

On - ly to fly a - way, _____

On - ly to fly as day

flies from moon - light. _____

Verse

So clear and deep are my fan - cies ____ ____ Of things I wish ____ were true. _____ I'll keep re - mem - b'ring eve - nings ____ I wish I'd spent with you. _____ I'll keep re -

A WONDERFUL GUY

Lyrics by OSCAR HAMMERSTEIN II
Music by RICHARD RODGERS

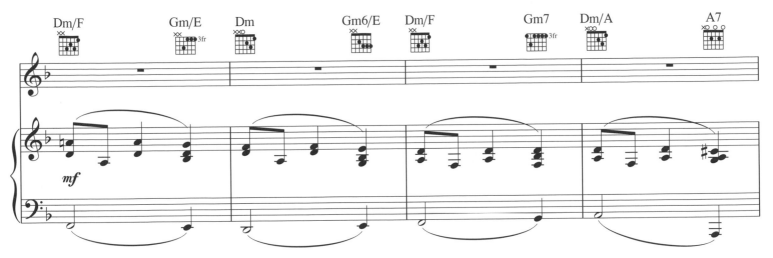

And they'll

say I'm na - ive As a babe to be - lieve An - y

fa - ble I hear from a per - son in pants.

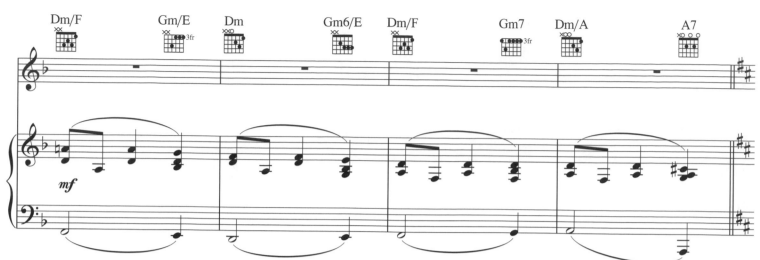

Fear - less - ly I'll face them and ar - gue their

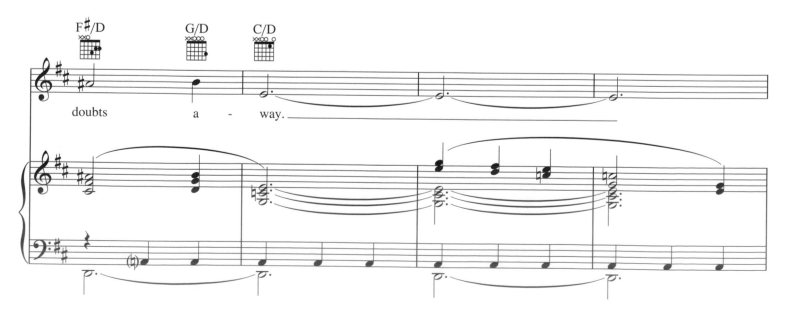

doubts a - way.

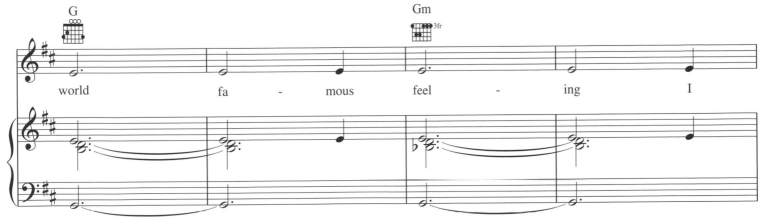

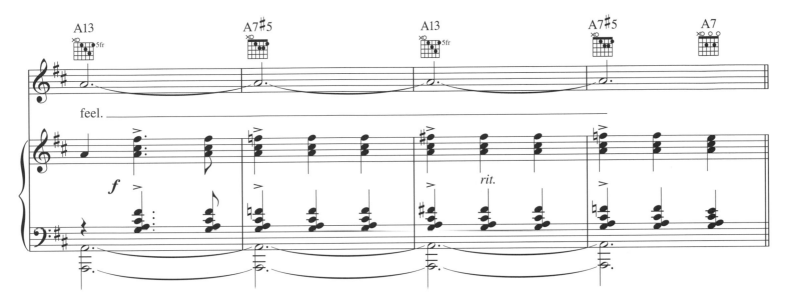

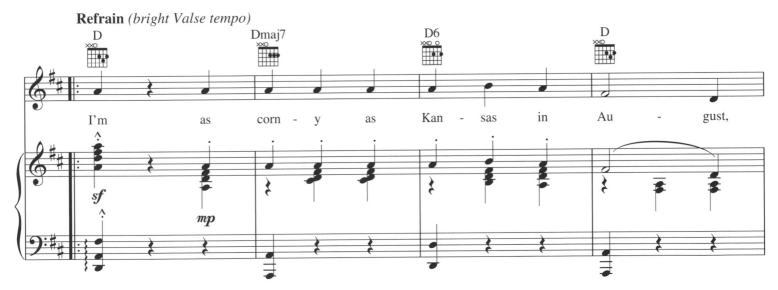

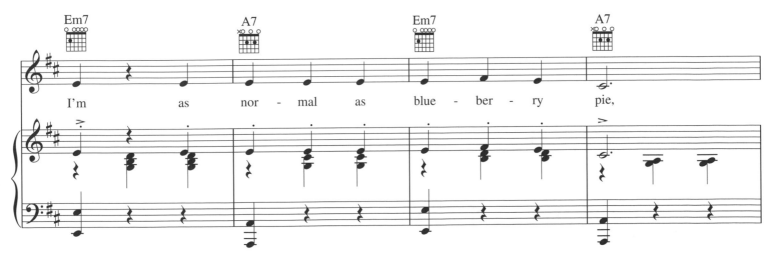

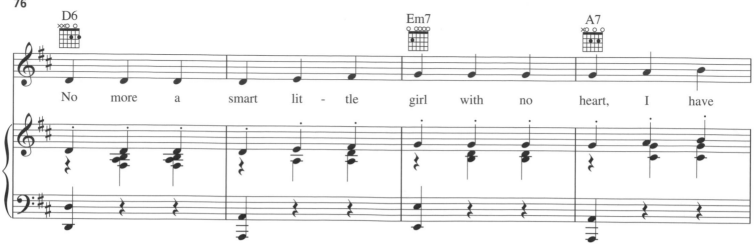

No more a smart lit - tle girl with no heart, I have

found me a won - der - ful guy! _____

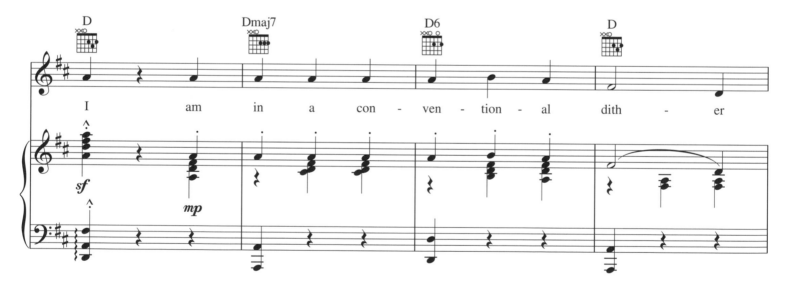

I am in a con - ven - tion - al dith - er

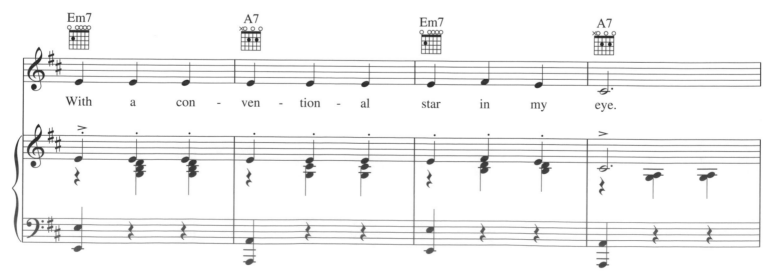

With a con - ven - tion - al star in my eye.

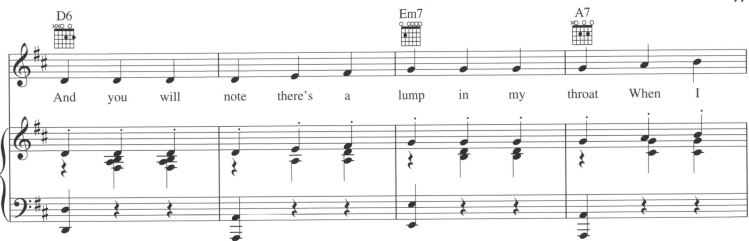

And you will note there's a lump in my throat When I

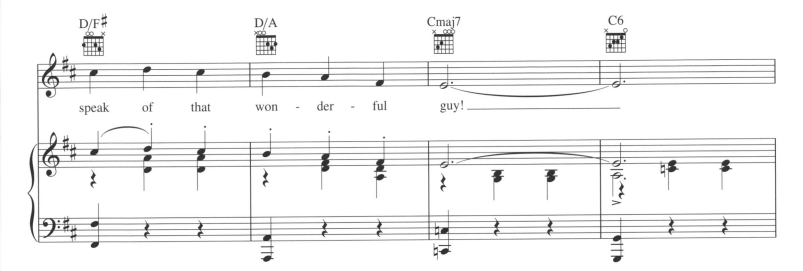

speak of that won - der - ful guy! _____

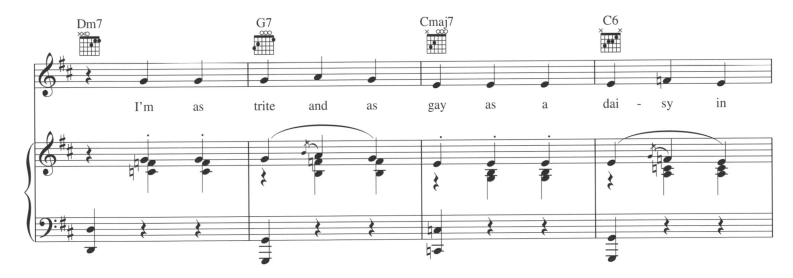

I'm as trite and as gay as a dai - sy in

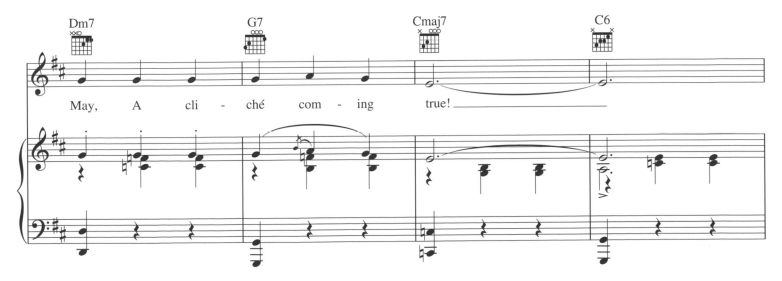

May, A cli - ché com - ing true! _____

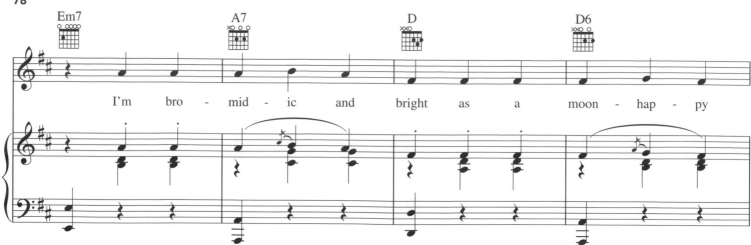

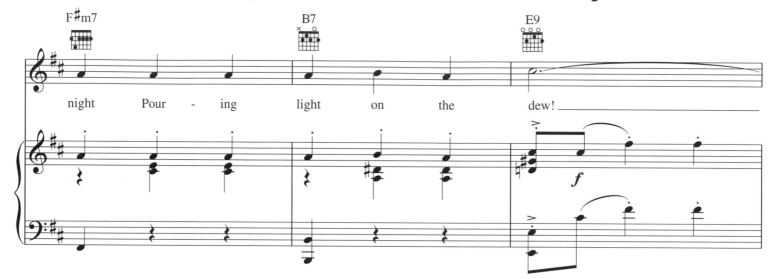

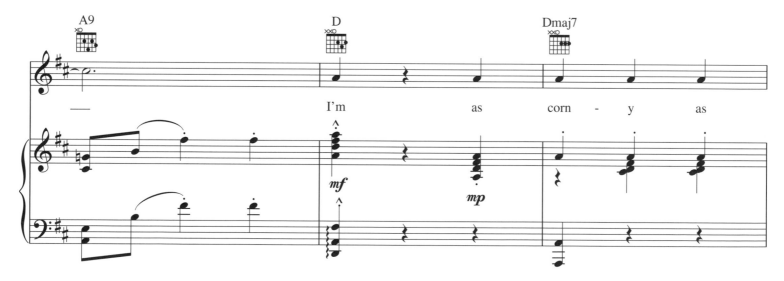

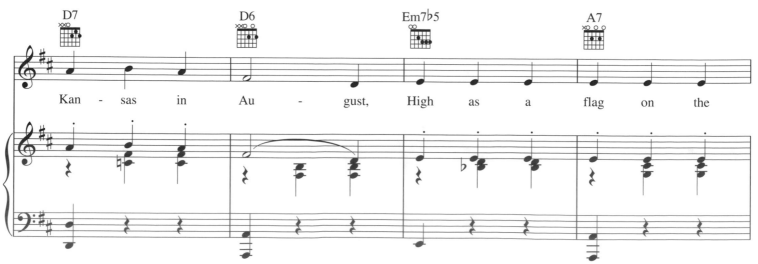

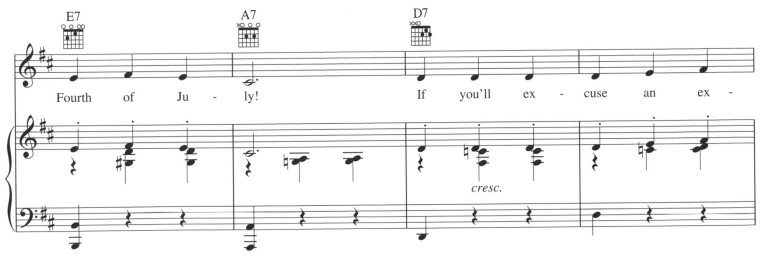

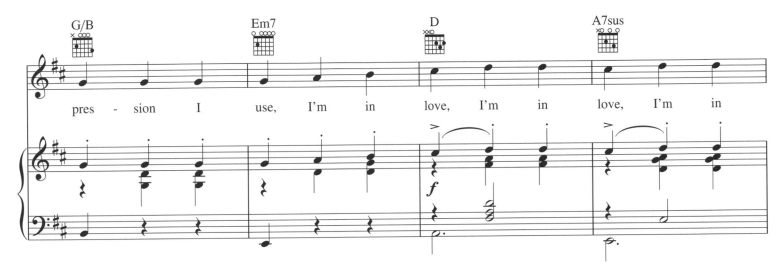

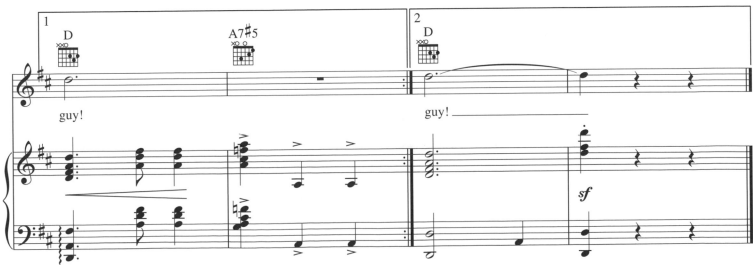

YOU'VE GOT TO BE CAREFULLY TAUGHT

Lyrics by OSCAR HAMMERSTEIN II
Music by RICHARD RODGERS

dear lit - tle ear. You've got to be

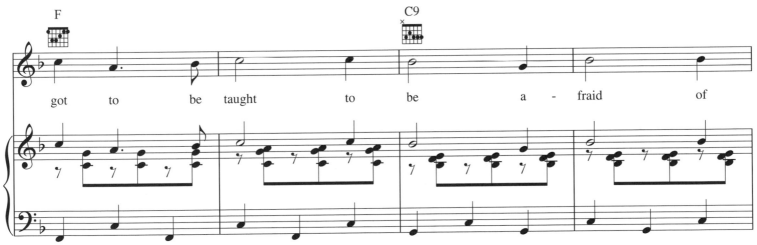

care - ful - ly taught. _____ You've

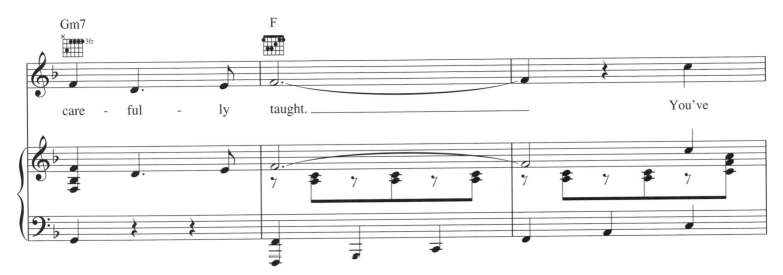

got to be taught to be a - fraid of

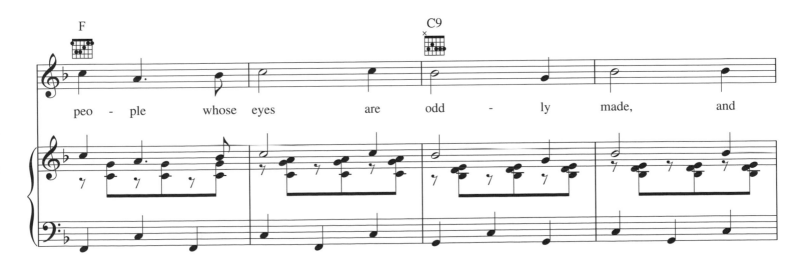

peo - ple whose eyes are odd - ly made, and

peo - ple whose skin is a dif - f'rent

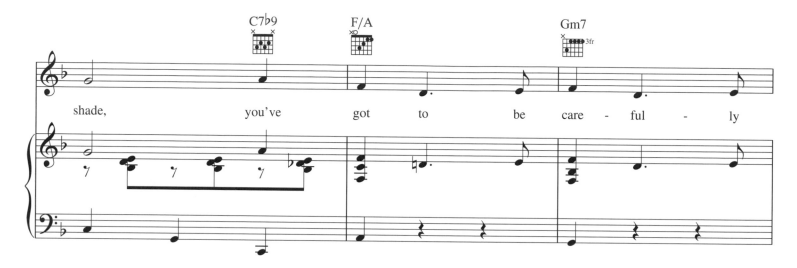

shade, you've got to be care - ful - ly

taught. _____ You've got to be taught be -

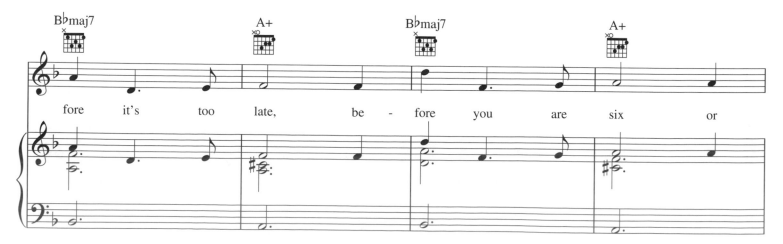

fore it's too late, be - fore you are six or

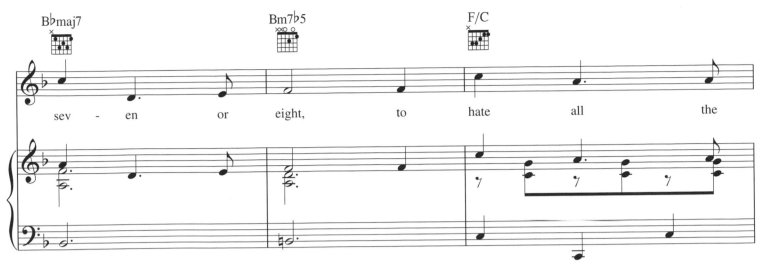

sev - en or eight, to hate all the

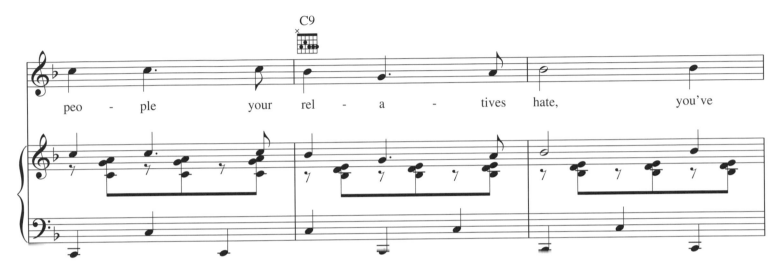

peo - ple your rel - a - tives hate, you've

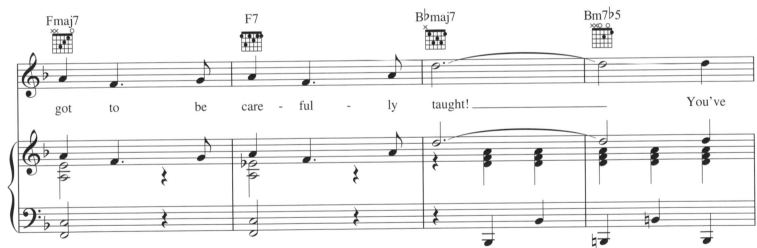

got to be care - ful - ly taught! _____ You've

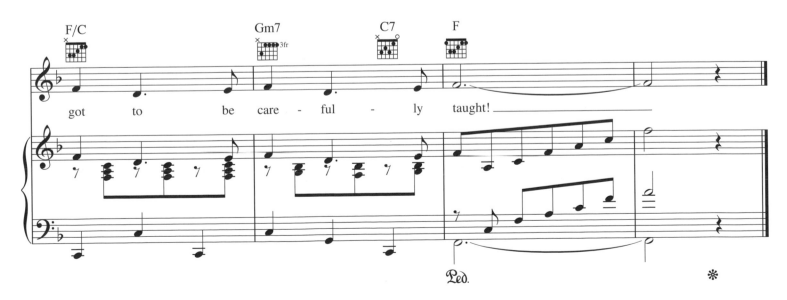

got to be care - ful - ly taught! _____

Ped. *

YOUNGER THAN SPRINGTIME

Lyrics by OSCAR HAMMERSTEIN II
Music by RICHARD RODGERS

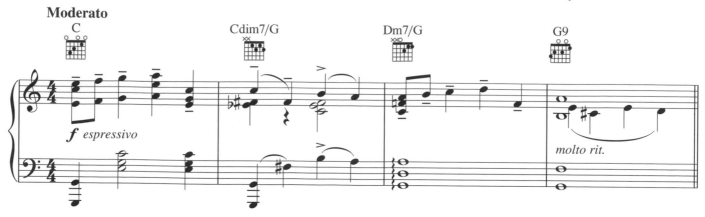

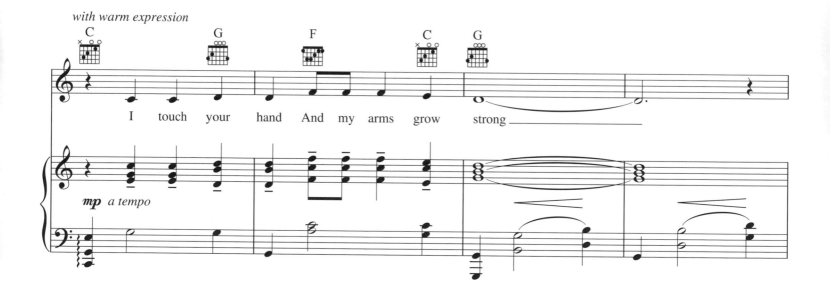

I touch your hand And my arms grow strong ___

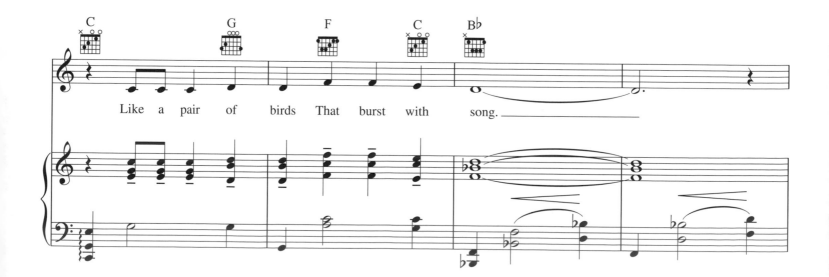

Like a pair of birds That burst with song. ___

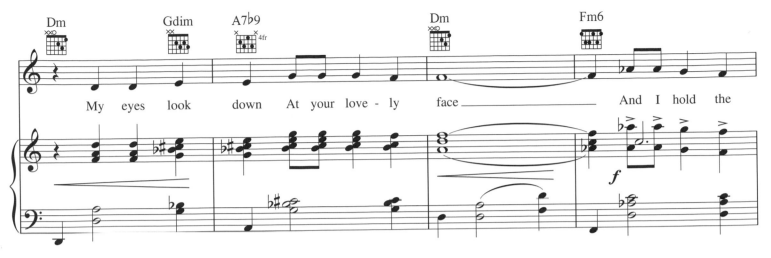

My eyes look down At your love-ly face _____ And I hold the

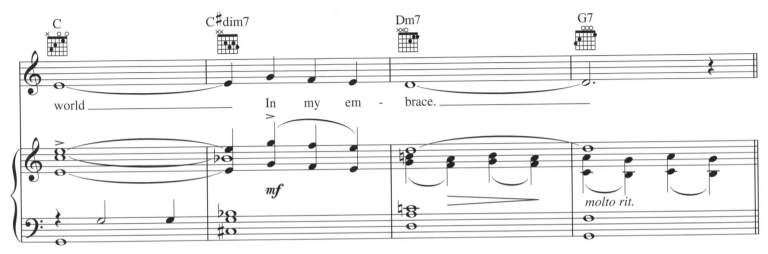

world _____ In my em - brace. _____

Refrain (*slowly, with great warmth*)

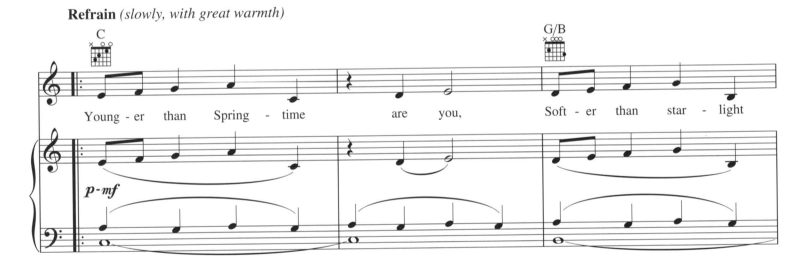

Young - er than Spring - time are you, Soft - er than star - light

are you, Warm - er than winds of June are the gen - tle lips you

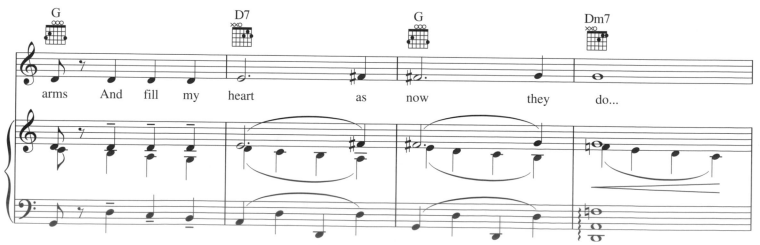

RODGERS AND HAMMERSTEIN™
VOCAL SELECTIONS

ALLEGRO
HL00312007 . . . .$10.95
Come Home • A Fellow Needs a Girl • The Gentleman Is a Dope • Money Isn't Ev'rything • So Far • You Are Never Away

CAROUSEL
HL01121008 . . . .$10.95
If I Loved You • June Is Bustin' Out All Over • Mister Snow • A Real Nice Clambake • Soliloquy • What's the Use of Wond'rin' • When the Children Are Asleep • You'll Never Walk Alone

CINDERELLA
HL00312091 . . . .$10.95
Boys and Girls Like You and Me • Cinderella March • Cinderella Waltz • Do I Love You Because You're Beautiful? • Impossible • In My Own Little Corner • Loneliness of Evening • A Lovely Night • Stepsisters' Lament • Ten Minutes Ago

FLOWER DRUM SONG
HL00313225 . . . .$12.95
Chop Suey • Don't Marry Me • Fan Tan Fannie • Grant Avenue • A Hundred Million Miracles • I Am Going to Like It Here • I Enjoy Being a Girl • Love, Look Away • My Best Love • Sunday • You Are Beautiful

THE KING AND I
HL00312227 . . . .$14.95
Getting to Know You • Hello, Young Lovers • I Have Dreamed • I Whistle a Happy Tune • The March of the Siamese Children • My Lord and Master • A Puzzlement • Shall I Tell You What I Think • Shall We Dance? • Something Wonderful • We Kiss in a Shadow • Western People Funny

ME AND JULIET
HL00312256 . . . .$10.95
The Big Black Giant • I'm Your Girl • It's Me • Keep It Gay • Marriage Type Love • No Other Love • That's the Way It Happens • A Very Special Day

OKLAHOMA!
HL00312292 . . . .$14.95
All Er Nothin' • The Farmer and the Cowman • I Cain't Say No • Kansas City • Lonely Room • Many a New Day • Oh, What a Beautiful Mornin' • Oklahoma • Out of My Dreams • People Will Say We're in Love • Pore Jud • The Surrey with the Fringe on Top

PIPE DREAM
HL00312320 . . . .$10.95
All at Once You Love Her • All Kinds of People • Everybody's Got a Home But Me • The Man I Used to Be • The Next Time It Happens • Suzy Is a Good Thing • Sweet Thursday

THE SOUND OF MUSIC
HL00312392 . . . .$10.95
Climb Ev'ry Mountain • Do-Re-Mi • Edelweiss • I Have Confidence • The Lonely Goatherd • Maria • My Favorite Things • Sixteen Going On Seventeen • So Long, Farewell • Something Good • The Sound of Music

SOUTH PACIFIC
HL00312400 . . . .$14.95
Bali Ha'i • Bloody Mary • A Cock-Eyed Optimist • Dites-Moi (Tell Me Why) • Happy Talk • Honey Bun • I'm Gonna Wash That Man Right Outa My Hair • My Girl Back Home • Some Enchanted Evening • There Is Nothin' Like a Dame • This Nearly Was Mine • Twin Soliloquies (This Is How It Feels) • A Wonderful Guy • You've Got to Be Carefully Taught • Younger Than Springtime

STATE FAIR
HL00312403 . . . .$10.95
All I Owe Ioway • Isn't It Kinda Fun • It Might As Well Be Spring • It's a Grand Night for Singing • It's the Little Things in Texas • More Than Just a Friend • Never Say "No" • Our State Fair • That's for Me • This Isn't Heaven • Willing and Eager

COMPLETE VOCAL SCORES also available!

HAL•LEONARD® CORPORATION
7777 W. BLUEMOUND RD. P.O. BOX 13819 MILWAUKEE, WI 53213